THE UNSTOPPABLE LEADER

DR. MARIO D. WALLACE

© Copyright 2020 by Mario D. Wallace, DBA

All rights reserved. No part of this publication may be reproduced, distributed, or transmitted in any form or by any means, including photocopying, recording, or electronic or mechanical methods, without the prior written permission of the publisher, except in the case of brief quotations embodied in critical reviews and certain other noncommercial uses permitted by copyright law. For permission requests, write to the publisher, addressed "Attention: Permissions Coordinator," at the address below.

All Things Strategic
PO Box 55661
Little Rock, Arkansas 72215
Allthingsstrategic.biz
Allthingsstrategic@gmail.com

Researcher and Editor: Holly Skinner, *www.hollyskinnerva.com*
Interior designer: Najdan Mancic, *www.iskonbookdesign.com*
Exterior Cover designer: Robert Harris, *www.vytocor.com*

Wallace, Mario D.
ISBN: 978-0-578-66359-3

This book is dedicated to my late mother and father, Deborah Ann Wallace, and Elias Muhammad. My mother always encouraged me to believe in myself and to pursue life with a passion while conquering my fears. My father instilled in me the passion for education and life learning. I really miss them.

I also dedicate this book to my children for their patience with me throughout my 10-year educational journey. My children are the rock and they keep me grounded and motivated to accomplish my life goals. Lastly, I dedicate this book to Orange Mound, the community where I was born and raised. Without the life experiences that I learned and earned in the Mound, I would not be the person I am today. Three fingers down and two fingers round.

CONTENTS

Strategic Frameworks 3

- SWOT Analysis 5
- Porter's Five Forces 7
- GE McKinsey Matrix 9
- BCG Growth Matrix 11
- Balanced Scorecard 13
- PEST Analysis 15
- Value Chain Analysis 17
- Generic Strategies 19
- Resource-based theory 21
- Disruptive Innovation 22
- Blue Ocean Strategies 24
- Platform Strategies 26
- TOWS Analysis 28
- SIPOC 30
- Fishbone Analysis 31
- Value Stream Mapping 33
- Affinity Diagram 35
- Process Mapping 37
- 5S 39
- Tree Diagram 41
- 8 Deadly Waste (WORMPIIT) 42
- Spaghetti Diagram 44
- Pareto Chart 45
- Failure Mode Effect Analysis (FMEA) 47
- Radar Chart 49
- Interrelationship Matrix 51
- ADEM Strategy Management Cyclical Model 53

Time Horizons Cone 55
Review Questions 57
About the Author 60
Our Consulting Services.. 62
Our Products... 67

OVERVIEW

Leaders have always yearned for a set of comprehensible and valuable leadership resources that could help them make sound business decisions and provide competitive business solutions. They have desired resources that help them effectively scan market environments, identify opportunities, create competitive strategic plans, mitigate threats, reduce wasteful expenditures, increase process efficiencies, and scale and grow their business. They have always wanted access to valuable information, frameworks, instruments, and tools to help them interpret complex data and make optimal business decisions for a firm. But until now, there has never been such a valuable pool of resources available for leaders to help them in both strategic and operational capacities.

The Unstoppable Leader is a treasure trove of industry changing strategic frameworks and operational tools, meant to enhance a leader's strategic and operational capabilities and to help them make informed business decisions.

The Unstoppable Leader is a practical guide and toolkit for leaders who desire to be dynamic and competitive in their approach to business solutions. The book introduces leaders to strategic frameworks and operational tools to help them determine the best competitive approach for any business. Leaders also learn the history, purpose, and application of some of these frameworks and tools, used by top business strategists and process improvement practitioners.

The purpose of this book is to help leaders make informed business decisions for any strategic or operational activity.

This book contains 28 frameworks with illustrations and elements to promote understanding.

All the chapters in the book provide leaders with history, description, and application of a strategic framework and/or operational tool. The appendix includes review questions for leaders to test their knowledge and understanding of the frameworks in this book.

Strategic Frameworks

SWOT ANALYSIS

```
              SWOT Analysis

   |  Strengths     |   Opportunities  |
   |----------------|------------------|
   |  Weaknesses    |   Threats        |
```

The SWOT Analysis was created by Albert Humphrey in the 1960's, when Humphrey was evaluating reasons for corporate failure. This analysis challenges corporations to look at planning from a holistic perspective. The analysis shifts planning from a solely internal process, to a process that also evaluates external and future factors that can impact a corporation.

SWOT stands for STRENGTHS, WEAKNESSES, OPPORTUNITIES, and THREATS. These four areas all need to be evaluated in the corporate planning process to truly understand the market in which the business wishes to excel. "STRENGTHS" are areas in which the business currently excels and factors that help contribute to success. For example, a business could recognize currents strengths such as "highly educated staff" or "ideal location". "WEAKNESSES" are the areas in which a business is struggling and can improve. For example, a business could have weaknesses including "inadequate staffing" or "limited marketing budget". "OPPORTUNITIES" are the areas in which there is room to improve and the current environment is right for improvement and growth. A sample business opportunity could include "increased philanthropy budget" or "new technology system". "THREATS" are factors that threaten to limit or decrease a company's success. For example, a threat could be "new local competitor" or "decreased budget". Through evaluating all the above, SWOT, a business is better equipped to make well informed decisions and better position themselves for success.

PORTER'S FIVE FORCES

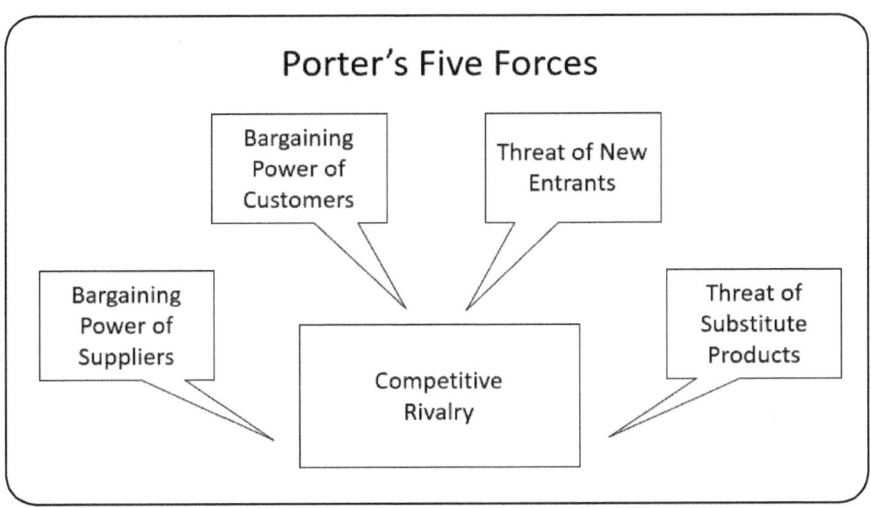

Developed in 1979, Porter's 5 Forces was developed by Michael Porter of Harvard University. Porter used industrial organization economics concepts to develop the 5 forces, which he states are the five forces that analyze market and competition of a business. These forces form what Porter called a "micro-environment" in which the organization will be working and serving customers. The five forces Porter identified are Threat of New Entrants, Threat of Substitution, Supplier Power, Buyer Power, and Competition/Industry Rivalry.

"Threat of New Entrants" refers to the growth rate of the industry and the threat of increased new competition. The level of threat posed by new entrants is determined by factors known as barriers to entry and include factors such as capital requirements, customer loyalty, and government policy. The second force, "Threat of Substitution" refers to the threat of competitors who are not direct competitors, but rather provide a completely different, substitute offering to a business's client base. This threat is increased as development speed increases and technology advances and is impacted by factors such as substitute cost and customer loyalty. The third force is "Supplier Power" and Porter identified this force as the power of suppliers to influence prices within the industry, due to supplier power to provide or limit materials or services. Suppliers often have a high level of bargaining power, particularly if they supply a material or service for which there is no substitute. A fourth force that impacts the market is "Buyer Power". This force refers to the negotiating power of the buyer, as the buyer creates the demand. Buyer power depends on variables such as how many options there are within a market and price sensitivity. The final force identified by Porter is "Competition" or "Industry Rivalry". The higher the rivalry within a market, the more competition there is for a limited number of customers. This factor can lead to decreased prices and increased advertising, as companies compete for the same customers.

GE MCKINSEY MATRIX

GE McKinsey Matrix

Business Units Strength

Market Attractiveness		High	Medium	Low
	High	Invest	Invest	Protect
	Medium	Invest	Protect	Harvest
	Low	Invest	Harvest	Divest

The GE Matrix was developed by McKinsey & Company consulting firm in the 1970s. The matrix compares a business's strength to the market. It is a way of evaluating which products and services should be offered, based on business strength and market attractiveness. This matrix is like the BCG matrix, in that it presents a large amount of data in a simplified manner.

"Market Attractiveness" is a subjective measure, and can depend on factors such as market growth, number of competitors, and bargaining power. "Business Strength" is also subjective and can be determined by looking at factors such as market share and customer loyalty. The GE Matrix is created using a 9-block chart. This chart places "Market

Attractiveness" on the vertical axis, with ranges from Low to High. "Business Strength" is placed on the horizontal axis and has the same three ranges. Divisions of the business are then placed into the matrix, based on where the intersection of market attractiveness and business strength occurs. Where divisions fall within the matrix allows business decision makers to determine whether to build a strategy, maintain a strategy, shrink a strategy etc. These various decision points and where they occur within the matrix are illustrated below. Business units with high market attractiveness and high business strength have the best chance for success and warrant investment. Conversely, those with low market attractiveness and low business strength should be divested. Therefore, the GE matrix allows for well-informed strategic decision making.

BCG GROWTH MATRIX

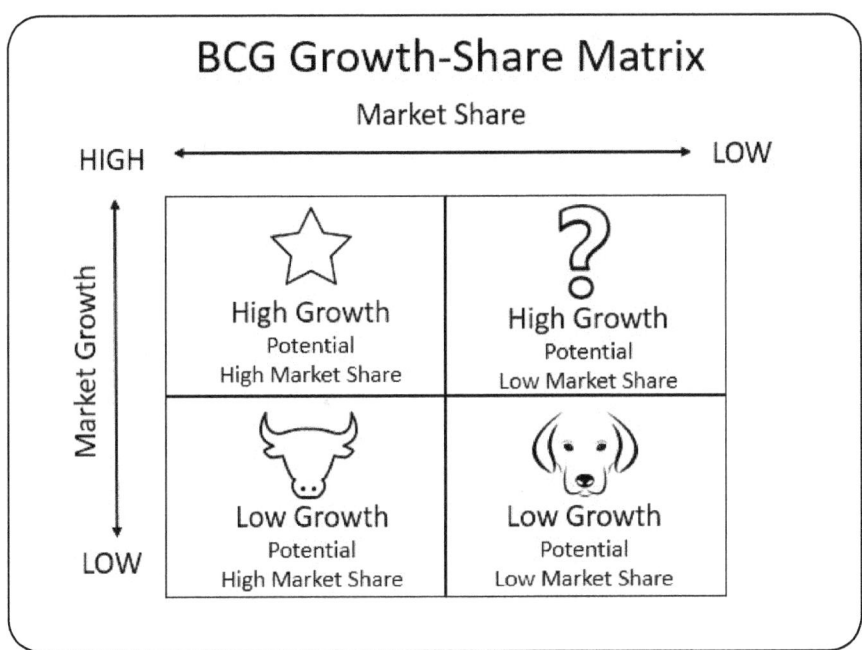

Like the GE Matrix, the BCG matrix evaluates multiple business units. By evaluating growth and share, the units are plotted on the matrix according to market growth and market share. The potential grid locations include "Cash Cow", "Star", "Question Mark", and "Dog". "Cash Cow" refers to a business unit with has a potential low growth rate and high market share.

This successful unit requires few resources or investment and grows over time. The "Question Mark" is one with high growth rate, but potentially low market share. These units are riskier and require more resources in order to increase market share, therefore, require both investment and divesting. The "Star"

Strategic Frameworks | 11

is a unit with high growth rate and high market share. This is a unit that requires investment, but also has potentially high returns. The "Dog" is a unit that has a low growth rate and low market share. This section of the matrix usually represents units that are tying up resources and need to be divested. This matrix was developed in the 1970s by the Boston Consulting Group.

BALANCED SCORECARD

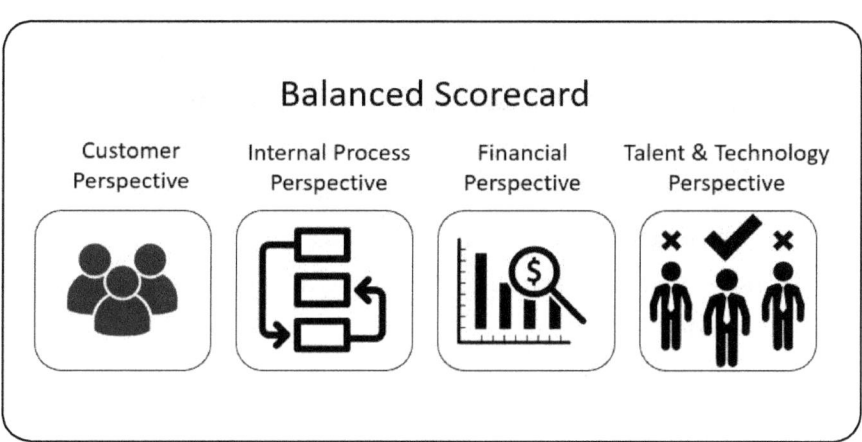

The Balanced Scorecard is a way to monitor strategic performance. Developed in 1992 by Robert Kaplan and David Norton, the Balanced Scorecard evaluates performance across four separate perspectives. These include financial, customer, learning and growth, and internal business process. The Balanced Scorecard should take place at the beginning of any strategic management, as it allows a clear understanding of internal and external factors that will influence the business. Each aspect of the scorecard is driven by objectives, which are evaluated by measures with set targets, and the initiatives needed to reach these targets and fulfill each objective. The scorecard helps connect overall strategic vision to day to day processes.

The financial component of the scorecard details what is needed in order to succeed financially, including use of resources and overall financial performance. The internal business process component details the processes which much be fulfilled successfully in order to have overall strategic success, such as the level of quality needed. The customer component evaluates how the business should appear to the customer and includes measures such as customer satisfaction. Finally, the innovation and learning details what training, human resources, and skills are required to change over time and continually improve as a business. Together these perspectives drive a business to successfully fulfill its strategic goals, which are driven by the Mission, Vision, and Values of the business.

PEST ANALYSIS

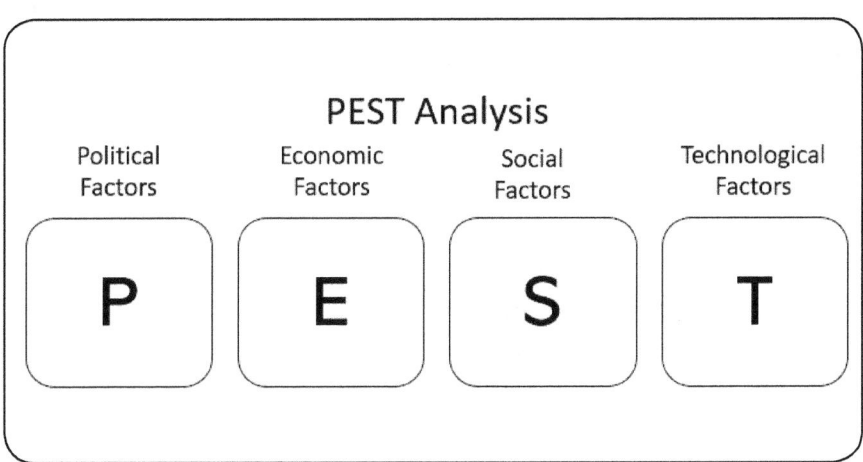

For more than 53 years, the go to environmental scan instrument has been the PEST analysis. Created by Dr. Francis Aguilar in 1967, the PEST analysis was one of the foundational tools for strategic planning. In Dr. Aguilar's novel *Scanning the Business Environment*, he identified four factors that influenced market dynamics. These factors were political, economic, socio-cultural, and technological.

Although the original acronym for the PEST analysis was ETPS, other scholars assisted in arranging the letters in the acronym to make the factors easy to remember. Political factors to consider include current and pending regulations, upcoming elections, and overall political climate. Economic factors include economic stability, unemployment rate, and consumer behaviors. Social factors could include population rates, generational patterns, and lifestyle choices. Technological factors include technological advances or changes in infrastructure. With all these factors being examined at a macro-level, each factor has the potential to have a positive or negative influence on the business. Therefore, this analysis provides a broad view of the current overall climate and allows for a "birds-eye view" of the environment.

VALUE CHAIN ANALYSIS

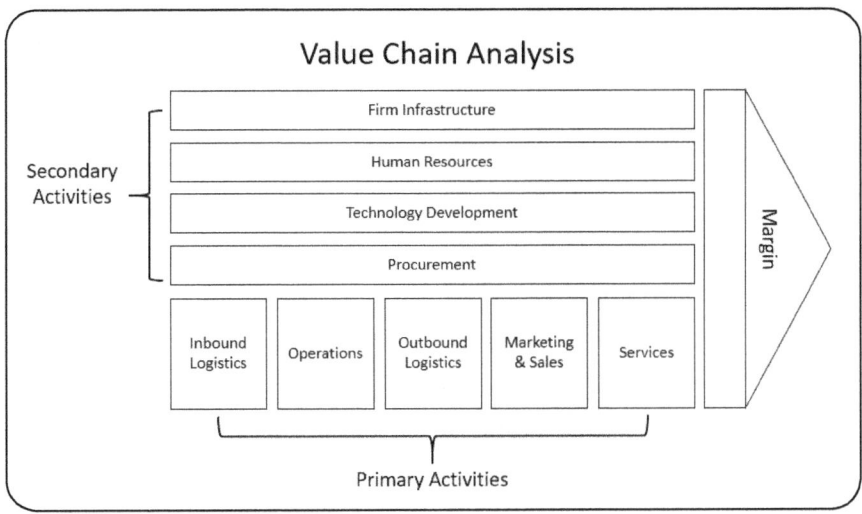

The Value Chain Analysis strategy framework was introduced in 1985 by Michael Porter. Porter identified a value chain as the activities carried out by a business in order to bring value to a customer. In summary, the value chain analyzes how a business take inputs and uses these inputs to create a more valuable output. Porter focused on systems with this analysis and focused on both primary activities and support activities.

Porter identified five primary activities which directly lead to creation of a product or delivery of a service. These primary activities include inbound logistics, operations, outbound logistics, marketing and sales, and service. Inbound logistics refer to processes related to supplies and inputs, including receiving and storage whereas outbound logistics refer to the logistics of the outputs, including delivery and distribution.

Operations refers to what happens in order to convert inputs into outputs, including product creation. Marketing and sales are the activities which influence potential clients to buy your product or service and includes advertising and sales campaigns. Service describes maintenance of value once a client has purchased from you and includes client relations and communication.

Porter also identified four support activities, which must occur in order for the primary activities to be able to occur successfully. These include procurement, human resource management, technological development, and infrastructure. Procurement is the purchasing of necessary supplies in order to support operation and includes contract negotiation and price comparison. Human resource management is the management of human capital and involves recruiting, training, and motivating staff. Technological development refers to the activities related to managing information and includes staying up to date with modern technology. Infrastructure are the overall support systems that allow the business to function and include management and accounting functions. Without these support activities, the primary activities would be unable to occur, and the business would cease to function.

GENERIC STRATEGIES

```
                  Generic Strategies

                  Competitive Advantage

              ┌──────────────────┬──────────────────┐
   Broad      │                  │                  │
   Target     │  Cost Leadership │  Differentiation │
              │                  │                  │   Competitive
              ├──────────────────┼──────────────────┤   Scope
   Narrow     │      Cost        │  Differentiation │
   Target     │      Focus       │      Focus       │
              └──────────────────┴──────────────────┘
```

Generic Strategies refer to Michael Porter's description of a company's competitive advantage in the marketplace. Porter described four generic strategies for a company to set itself apart from competition, and believed businesses needed to look at both their competitive advantage and their competitive scope. He identified two types of competitive advantage that a company could pursue: lower cost or product/service differentiation. He also identified two types of scope: either narrow focused which targets a small market segment or broad which covers the entire market.

As this diagram illustrates, a business can either seek to offer the lowest cost to a broad market, can differentiate and offer to a broad market, can narrow their market but maintain lower cost, or have a narrow market and focus

Strategic Frameworks | 19

on differentiation. These possible combinations can assist strategists decide which combination of scope and advantage they want to offer, based upon target market and product/service uniqueness. Porter stressed that only one strategy could be focused on at a time, in order to avoid being "stuck in the middle". He stressed that trying to achieve more than one of the above strategies would cause lack of focus and, ultimately, inability to succeed.

RESOURCE-BASED THEORY

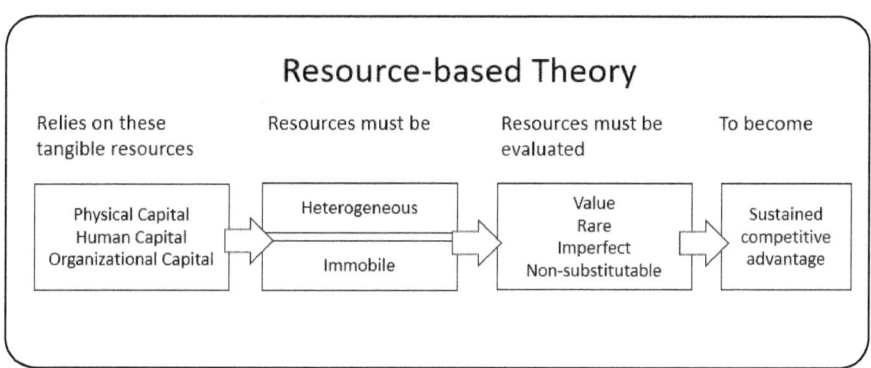

The research-based view, or RBV, was first developed in the 1980s through the work of Birger Wernerfelt and later expanded and further defined by Jay Barney in 1991. In contrast to other strategic frameworks, this framework focuses on the internal resources that can influence a business's market position.

According to Barney, resources can lead to a competitive advantage if the resources are Valuable, Rare, In-Imitable, and Nonsubstituable (VRIN). These characteristics all refer to resources that are not easily found or replicated. Therefore, the business in possession of such resources can stand apart from competition and maintain a competitive advantage. These resources can be either tangible or intangible but must have the "VRIN" characteristics in order to truly benefit a business and make it unique.

DISRUPTIVE INNOVATION

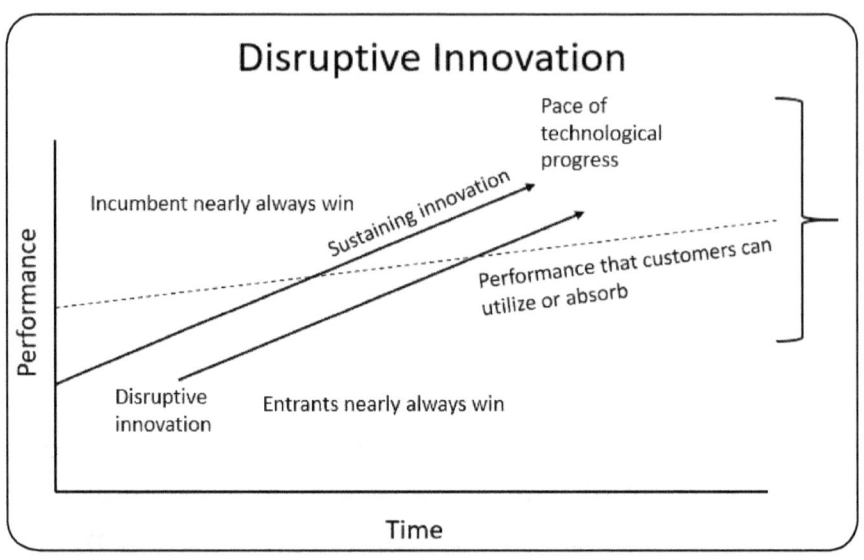

Disruptive innovation is a term developed by Clayton Christensen in 1995 and refers to a new market or market entrant that "disrupts" the existing market. Christenson argues that while new market entrants usually enter at the bottom of the market, overtime they continue to move up through the market and eventually disrupt established market leaders. Disruptive innovations usually involve more risk and are more likely developed by outside entrepreneurs than current market participants. In addition, these innovations may take a longer time to enter the market and truly "take off". However, once they enter the market, they have the tendency to disrupt the market and achieve faster and more wide-reaching impact on the established market. These disruptive innovations usually target new customer groups and often represent very "forward thinking" business concepts and products. In addition, these innovations typically target low-end and mainstream customers often overlooked by companies trying to focus only on high-end customers

BLUE OCEAN STRATEGIES

Blue Ocean Strategies	
Red Ocean Strategies	Blue Ocean Strategies
Compete in existing market space	Create uncontested market space
Beat the competition	Make the competition irrelevant
Exploit existing demand	Create and capture new demand
Make the value-cost-trade-off	Break the value-cost-trade-off
Align the whole system of a firm's activities with its strategic choice of differentiation or low cost	Align the whole system of a firm's activities in pursuit of differentiation and low cost

Blue Ocean Strategy was a book released by W.C. Kim and Renee Mauborgne in 2005. This book focused on ways to leverage core competencies in order to gain an edge in the market. The focus of this book was to look at the "blue ocean" of open competition area, instead of solely focusing on current competition. Through looking at "uncharted territory", businesses have a chance to expand their products and services in a way that greatly increases value. The Blue Ocean strategies are contrasted with the Red Ocean strategies, also known as the current marketplace or status quo.

Whereas the Red Ocean promotes competing in an existing market and learning to beat the current competition, the Blue Ocean advocates creating a completely new market. This strategy allows a business to, therefore, develop new demand and make current competition irrelevant. In addition, it eliminates the need to price compete or lower value. The Blue Ocean places a business in the driver's seat and allows them to set the value, instead of being solely reliant on the current market. This innovative strategic framework encourages businesses to be trailblazers and to work to chart previously uncharted territory.

PLATFORM STRATEGIES

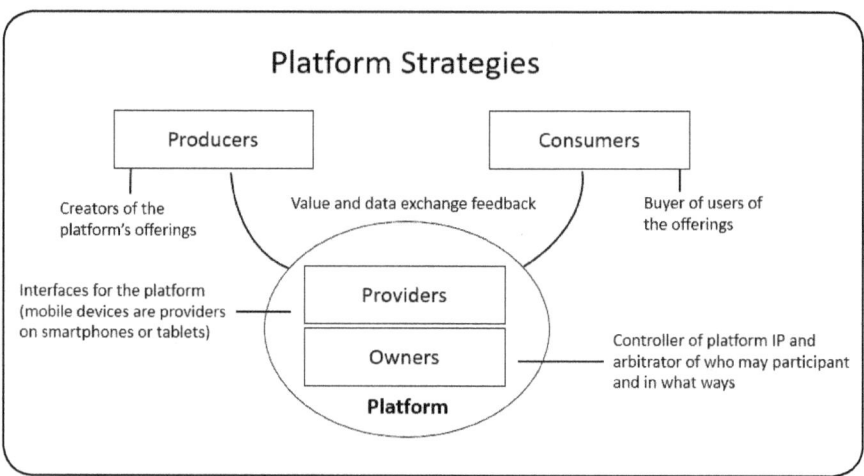

Platform strategies were introduced through the book "The Platform Revolution", written by Geoffrey Parker, Marshall Van Alstyne, and Sangeet Choudary. This strategy evaluates the impact of online platforms on various industries and the importance of harnessing the power of online platforms. As the marketplace continues to advance technologically, the use of online platforms becomes more necessary. Businesses from Uber to AirBNB all effectively utilize online platforms to grow and expand their market impact.

In order to succeed, appropriate markets must be identified and ways to monetize these markets must be developed. Platforms are used to facilitate interactions that create value, between producers and consumers. These platforms allow consumers to interact openly with the business and facilitate the exchange of products and services. Platforms consist of four different players: Owners, Providers, Consumers, and Producers. Owners provide the material, providers interface with users, producers create the material, and consumers use the materials.

TOWS ANALYSIS

TOWS Analysis			
INTERNAL FACTORS			
EXTERNAL FACTORS		Strengths (S)	Weaknesses (W)
	Opportunities (O)	Strengths/ Opportunities (SO)	Weaknesses/ Opportunities (WO)
	Threats (T)	Strengths/ Threats (ST)	Weaknesses/ Threats (WT)

TOWS Analysis is a strategic planning tool that evaluates the same factors as the SWOT analysis. The factors evaluated are still strengths, weaknesses, opportunities, and threats. However, these factors are evaluated in the reverse order of the SWOT analysis and threats and opportunities are evaluated first. This allows managers to gain an understanding of external factors before they get bogged down with internal analysis. Therefore, while the factors evaluated are the same, the order in which they are analyzed can lead to different results and different strategic conversations. Typically, the TOWS analysis allows strategic planning to be taken a step further and provides deeper insight than originally gained from the SWOT analysis by more closely evaluating internal and external factors.

The TOWS analysis creates four potential strategies: Strength/Opportunity (SO), Weakness/Opportunity (WO), Strength/Threat (ST), and Weakness/Threat (WT). SO strategy would use a business's strengths to increase opportunity and WO strategy would evaluate and work to eliminate weaknesses in order to increase opportunity. ST would use strengths to overcome any threats and WT would identify and downplay weaknesses in order to avoid threats.

SIPOC

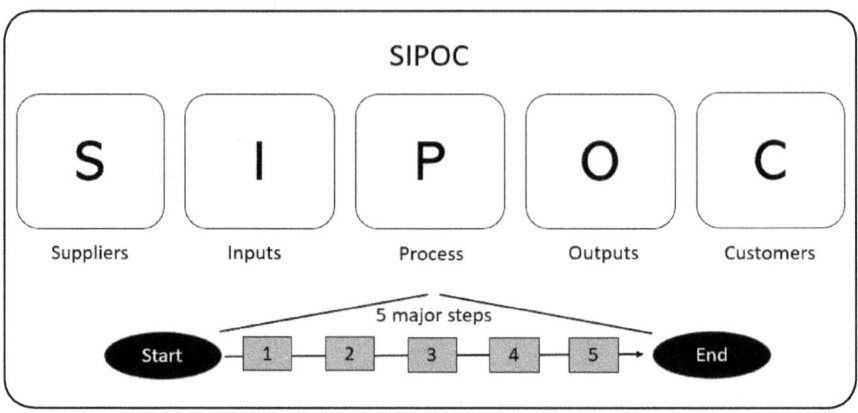

The SIPOC diagram is used in Six Sigma, a methodology developed by Bill Smith in 1985. This diagram is used to evaluate relevant components of a process improvement project. The elements include Suppliers, Inputs, Process, Outputs, and Customers. By evaluating each of these elements, process improvement projects are better planned before the work of improvement begins.

Suppliers can be internal or external and refer to the suppliers of inputs to the process being evaluated. Inputs are the resources or information consumed in the process and process is the steps that transform inputs into outputs. Outputs are the final product or service consumed by the customer. The customer refers to the person or company who receives the output of the process. By evaluating all these elements, complex processes can be better understood and managed.

FISHBONE ANALYSIS

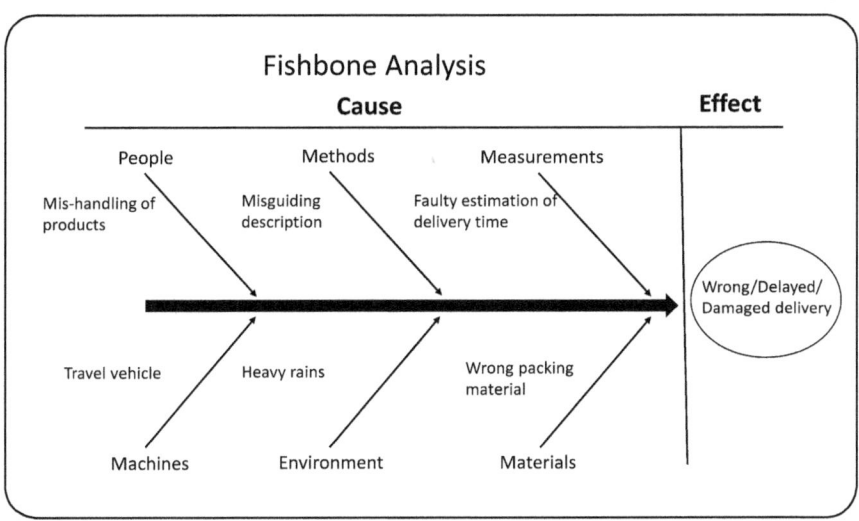

The Fishbone Analysis is an operational framework developed by Kaoru Ishikawa in 1990. The fishbone diagram is a cause and effect diagram that evaluates potential causes of a problem in order to find root causes. This diagram is particularly useful when a team is stuck and unable to easily identify causes of their problems.

To form a fishbone diagram, the problem being evaluated is listed as the head, with a backbone stemming from the head. Coming from this "backbone" are listed potential causes to the identified problem, evaluating areas such as people, environment, materials, management, equipment, and process. Around each of these potential causes are listed causes that contributed to that potential cause. This method allows each cause to be continually broken down and evaluated until root causes are identified. Using this diagram, teams can better address problems once the true root causes are known.

VALUE STREAM MAPPING

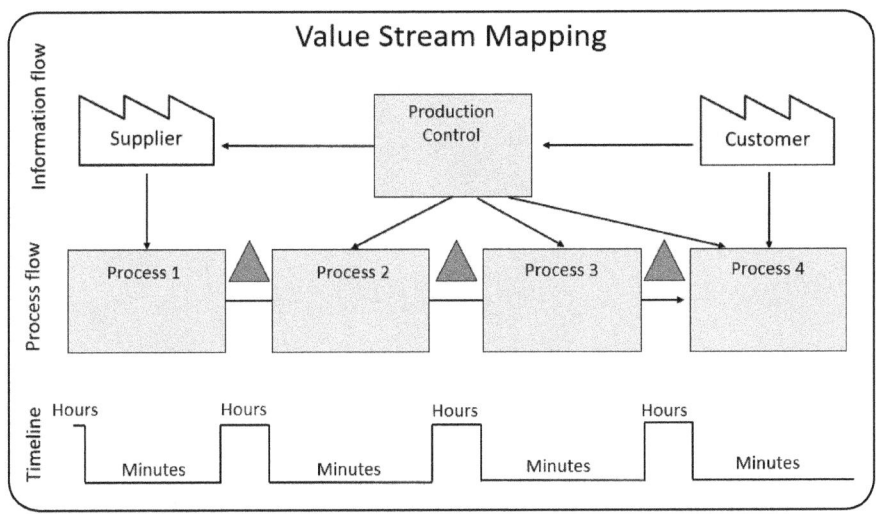

Value Stream Mapping is part of Lean Methodology developed by Toyota in the 1990s. This mapping is used to evaluate a process for waste and to identify which elements of a process truly add value. This helps lead a process to a truly lean state by eliminating activities that are wasteful.

Value Stream Mapping uses a variety of symbols to identify various work activities and the flow of information in the process being evaluated. Items mapped are evaluated for whether they truly add value to the overall process. The Value Stream Mapping typically involves mapping out the current process and then mapping out an ideal state. Through looking at all parts of the process, it becomes easier to see what elements are essential and which are wasteful and can be eliminated when trying to transform from current state to ideal future state. As part of looking at where waste may

Strategic Frameworks | 33

exist, it is suggested to use the mnemonic "CUT COSTS". Using this mnemonic, team members can evaluate the following and try and identify waste: cycle times, uptime available, total equipment, changeover time, operators, size of batches, time available, and shifts involved. These will not apply to every process, but are frequently an appropriate place to start, particularly for manufacturing processes.

AFFINITY DIAGRAM

Affinity diagrams are a way of organizing similar ideas and concepts according to similar themes. This method of grouping makes it easier to address common challenges and leads to more successful brainstorming sessions as focus becomes narrowed. It also allows the entire process to be looked at in a manageable fashion.

Affinity diagrams were first developed by Jiro Kawakita in the 1960s. These diagrams are particularly useful when evaluating a process in order to fix a problem. This grouping allows problems to be broken down into manageable pieces that can each be addressed in order to fix the whole process. Also, this grouping allows team members to objectively identify and group challenges, without hostile communication but rather "just the facts".

Unorganized elements

Strategic Frameworks

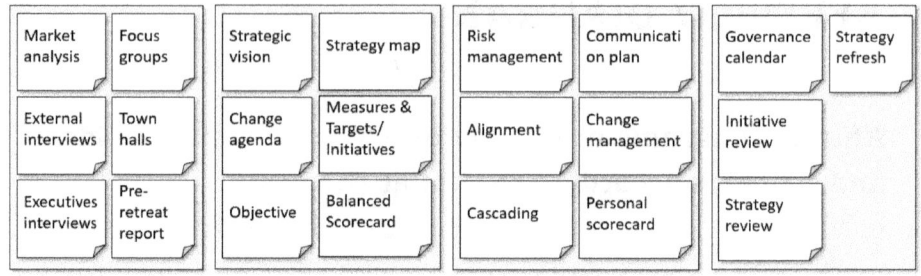

Organized elements

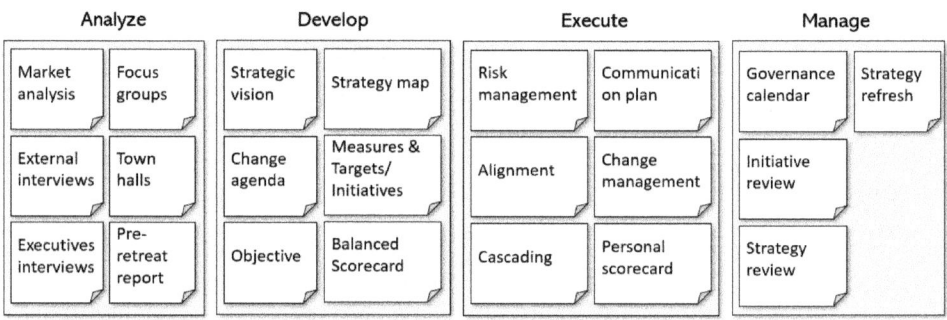

Naming elements grouped into affinities

PROCESS MAPPING

The operational framework of process mapping is creating a workflow diagram in order to get a better understanding of a process or series of processes. Process mapping was first developed by Frank Gilbreth in the early 1900s. The concept of process mapping can be used in a variety of industries, from manufacturing to sales to client relations.

Process mapping is essentially mapping a workflow to identify all steps in the process. The mapping details each step in a process and identifies who is responsible for successful completion of each step. Inputs, handoff points, outpoints, and decision points are all identified in process mapping. Through this mapping, bottlenecks can be identified, and steps being duplicated or done inefficiently can be identified and corrected. Various symbols are used throughout the mapping to identify decision points and outcomes. Overall, the mapping of a business's various processes through process mapping can lead to overall increased effectiveness and more streamlined, efficient processes.

PROCESS MAPPING

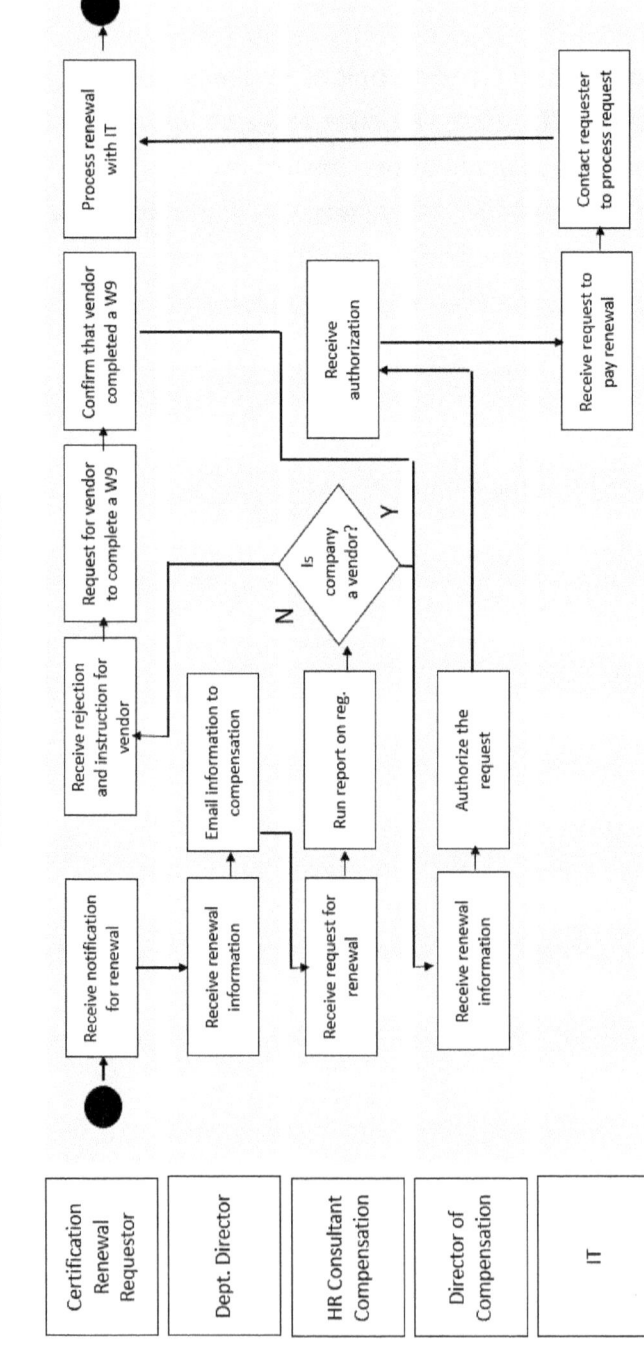

38 | THE UNSTOPPABLE LEADER

5S

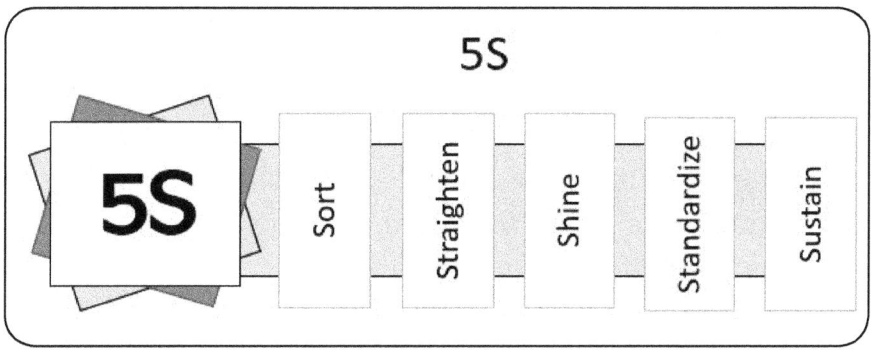

5S refers to an organization method originally developed by Toyota Manufacturing in the 1970s in order to increase efficiency and value. 5S stands for "Sort, Set, Shine, Standardize, and Sustain". These steps are applied to the workplace in order to increase organization and value, while decreasing waste.

Sort refers to sorting through a workplace in order to organize materials, equipment, furniture etc. This sorting looks at each item and evaluates it for value. It involves looking at each item and deciding when the item was last used, how often is it used, and does it need to be in this area. Set refers to looking at the remaining items after the sort, so those items that have been deemed necessary in the work area. Set involves placing items where they make the most sense based on who uses the item, how the item is used, and where the item is used. Set is essentially organizing the items in a workplace and storing them in a way that eliminates disorganization. One item is placed and organized where they belong, the next step is to Shine. This refers to cleaning the space based on the new storage arrangements. Shine also involves regular maintenance on equipment in the space, to prevent downtime. The next step is to Standardize. This refers to maintaining the new organization through regular upkeep, instead of allowing the new, clean space to slowly slip back into a state of disorganization. Using a checklist is often helpful to remind employees which steps to do on a regular basis to maintain the organized space. The final step is Sustain. This refers to maintaining the processes and updating as necessary. This involves keeping up employee enthusiasm and involvement for the project. Sustaining is necessary to ensure the new state of organization is maintained.

TREE DIAGRAM

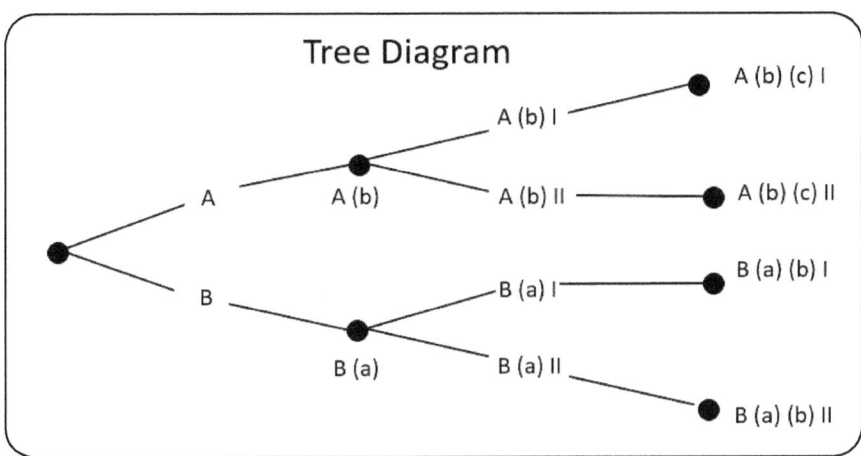

The tree diagram is an operational framework that takes a central idea and continues to branch this idea into more specific parts. This allows for a systematic approach to taking an idea from a general concept to specific components. This tool not only helps a team organize its thinking, but it is a quick way to visualize relationships between concepts and notice any patterns or problems.

The tree diagram was first developed by as part of Six Sigma methodology and can be used to organize a wide variety of processes. Tree diagrams can help identify the root causes of problems and can help problems become more manageable by looking at their component parts. For example, in the simple menu planning example below, each menu item is further broken down into options and component parts, making it easier to get a full picture and to recognize relationships between items.

Strategic Frameworks | 41

8 DEADLY WASTE (WORMPIIT)

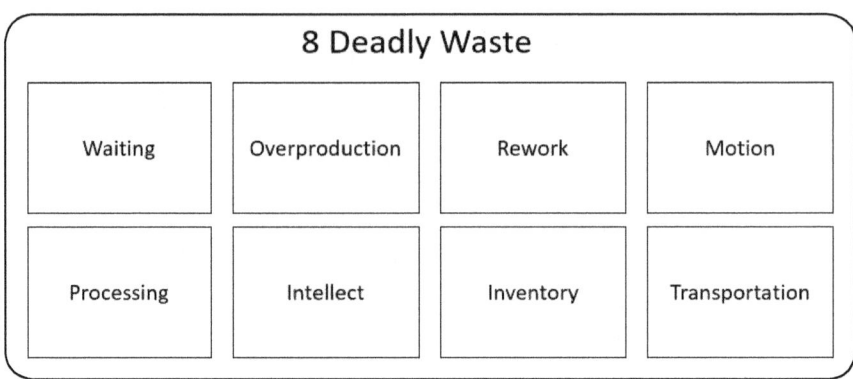

Lean methodology identifies 8 deadly wastes and ways to eliminate these forms of waste in the workplace. Developed at Toyota in the 1980s, Lean methodology has expanded into a way of increasing value to the customer, while reducing waste of time and resources. One of Lean's main ways to identify waste is using the 8 Deadly Waste guidelines.

The 8 deadly wastes of Lean methodology are identified as follows: Defects and scraps, overproduction, waiting, not utilizing talent, transportation, inventory, motion waste, excess processing. These 8 wastes make up the mnemonic "DOWNTIME". "Defects and scraps" refer to mistakes that require extra money and/or resources in order to correct. For example, a defective product that must be remade before being able to be used. Defects are often the result of internal issues such as unstandardized workflows, poor quality control, poor inventory control and more. Through identifying where defects are occurring, the process associated with creating the defective component can be further analyzed and ultimately corrected. "Overproduction" refers to producing more than is necessary to meet demand. This often means companies keep producing and ultimately wasting the extra products. Overproduction can be due to issues such as faulty market analysis, unawareness of customer needs, and failure to forecast. "Waiting" refers to anytime that work must stop, and production is placed in a state of waiting. Some factors that could cause waiting include breakdown in assembly, poor communication, or inadequate staffing. "Not utilizing talent" refers to underutilizing employee skill sets and not maximizing employee productivity. This can be caused by issues such as poor training, employees not properly matched to their job duties, and lack of teamwork. "Transportation" is waste caused by having to move things around. Most common in manufacturing, transportation issues can include poor workspace layout and excessive steps in a process, causing more time to be spent getting from "Point A" to "Point B" than is necessary. "Inventory" in the concept of waste refers to excess inventory. Like overproduction, excess inventory is due to an unawareness of customer needs and, often, poor inventory tracking systems. "Motion Waste" refers to any extra movement that does not contribute to the value of the product or service. Like transportation, motion waste is often due to poor layout and is when workers are required to move more than is necessary in order to complete the task. Finally, "Excess Processing" refers to duplication of similar tasks and additional unnecessary steps in a process. This excess processing can refer to duplication of signatures on a form, duplication of data entry, or simply human error.

SPAGHETTI DIAGRAM

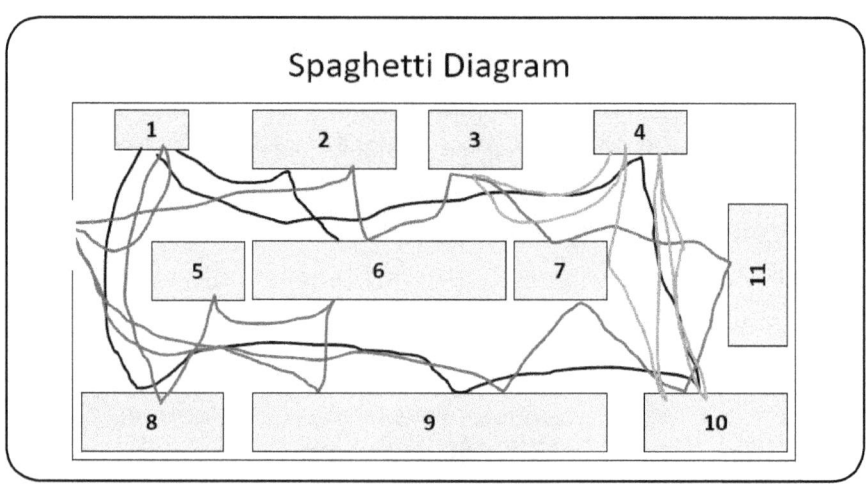

Spaghetti diagrams are an operational framework also part of the Lean methodology toolkit. The purpose of a spaghetti diagram is to analyze workflows. Using this diagram, a workflow is mapped from beginning to end, showing the people, information, and materials passed through the process.

Spaghetti diagrams are particularly useful for identifying waste and duplication in a process. In addition, spaghetti diagrams are usually an effective way to identify poor layouts in work areas. Evaluation of a completed spaghetti diagram helps a team conceptualize how to move from current state to future state. For example, in the spaghetti diagram below it is easy to spot areas of repetitive movement and inefficient flow. Each line represents a path of movement for either a person or a product. Therefore, using this information, the team can regroup and plan a new, improved future state with a better work area layout and more efficient communication channels.

PARETO CHART

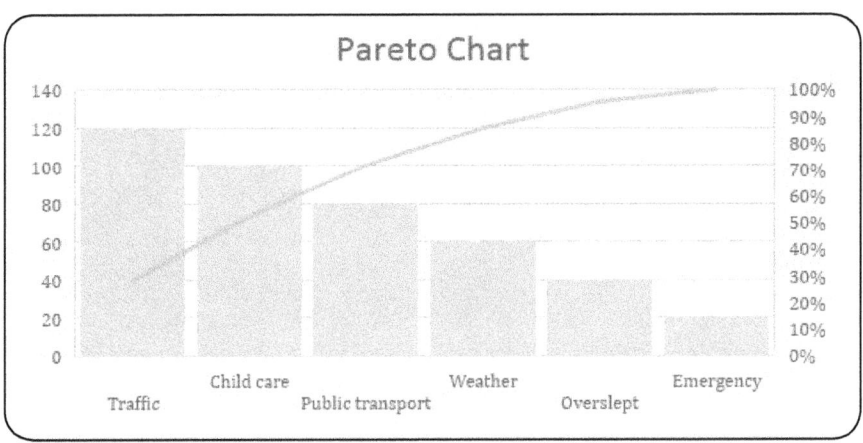

Vilfredo Pareto was the first to develop the Pareto chart in the early 1900s. Used throughout Lean/Six Sigma methodology, the Pareto Chart uses a bar graph with a line to depict varying levels of significance to elements of a process or problem being evaluated. Each bar on the graph represents a different component of the process or problem, and the height of each bar helps represent the significance of each factor. The value of each bar is presented in descending order, and a line placed on the graph represents the cumulative total of each bar. Pareto charts are an effective way to quickly and easily demonstrate levels of significance between groups of information. For example, in the Pareto Chart below, "reasons for lateness" were listed by frequency of response for each selection. As the pareto chart shows, the areas of most significance when it comes to tardiness in the respondents are traffic and childcare. In fact, if these two factors were corrected, 75% of the reasons for lateness would be corrected as shown by the line graph. Therefore, the Pareto Chart serves as an easy way to visualize areas of high significance and to, in response, plan interventions accordingly.

FAILURE MODE EFFECT ANALYSIS (FMEA)

Failure Mode Effect Analysis was developed in the early 1950s by engineers looking at reliability. FMEA is a useful tool for risk management and is a way to determine the risk associated with potential failures in a process or production. Typically, FMEA looks at either process or design. Three factors are used to evaluate the potential risk level of a process or design including the frequency of occurrence, the severity of the consequence if failure occurs, and the chance of detection of the failure.

Each of these factors contributes to the RPN, or risk priority number, which serves as a numerical indicator of potential risk associated with failure mode. The frequency of occurrence is a representation of estimated rates of failure, the severity is a measure of the potential impact of failure, and the chance of detection is how likely it is for this failure to be noticed. Through evaluating these factors, the product of each potential failure can be translated into an RPN and placed in order of significance according to level of projected risk. FMEA is a way for prioritizing projects and processes and serves to develop failure safeguards in order of highest priority and largest impact. For example, , the soap makers would be wise to safeguard against the potential failure of soap being too small or too big, since it has the highest risk. Therefore, they should work to prevent this failure, then the failure of wrong fragrance, and finally the failure of misshapen soap which has the lowest potential risk.

FAILURE MODE EFFECT ANALYSIS (FMEA)

Function/ Process	Potential Failure Mode	Potential Effects of Failure (s)	Severity Rating	Potential Causes of Failure (s)	Occurrence Rating	Current Process Controls	Detection Rating	Critical Characteristics	Risk Priority Number	Recommended Actions	Responsibility and Target Completion Data
	Mishappen Soap	>Mildly displeased customer	6	>Soap molds are old >Uncareful Workmanship >Soap molds are not regularly cleaned out	4	>None >Close Supervisor >None	1	N	24		
	Too small or too big in size	>Possible company losses	7	>Uncareful Workmanship >No uniform molds	3	>Close Supervisor >None	3	N	63	>Close supervision >Provide a uniform mold	>Factory Supervisor >General Manager
	Wrong fragrance	>Dissatisfied, possibly irked customers	10	>No standard Measurements >Mixers are not expert soap makers	3	>None >None	2	Y	60	>Standardize the procedure and Measurements >Hire an expert mixer	>Product Manager >General Manager

48 | THE UNSTOPPABLE LEADER

RADAR CHART

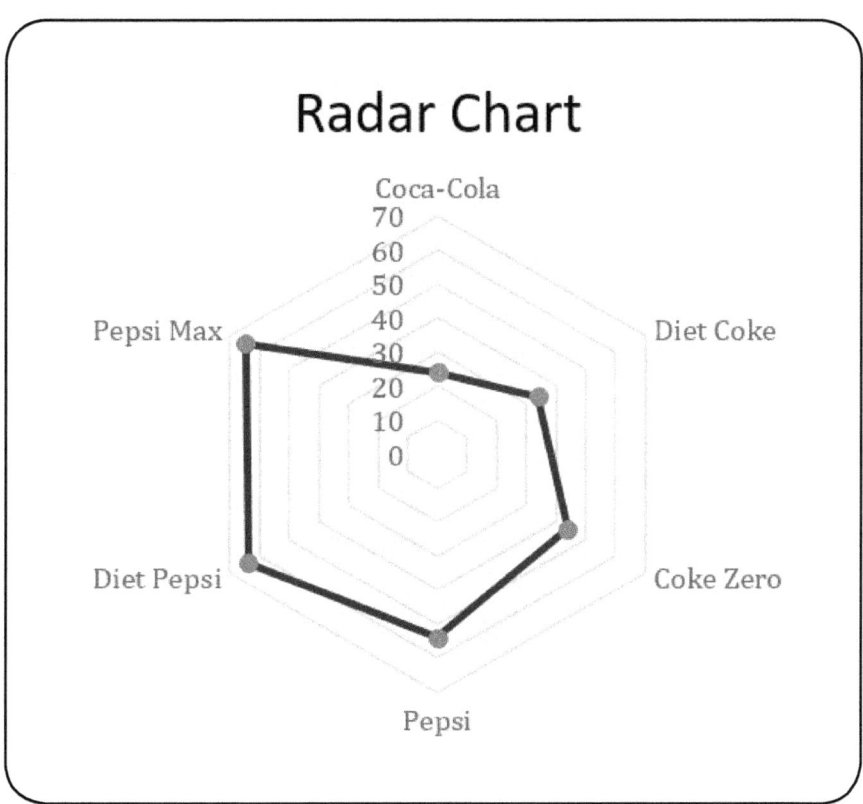

Radar charts are used to represent data sets with multiple variables in a graph with each variable originating from the same point. Each layer of the chart represents a different level of importance. Each data set is then graphed according to determined level of importance.

Each radar chart can have a different shape based on the number of factors being evaluated. However, the overall size of the radar chart is what drives the decision-making process.

The larger the chart, the more factors that reached the outer rings of the chart or the "highest desirable" characteristics. Smaller charts indicate that one or more factors has lower levels of desirable characteristics. While the overall decision will depend on the person or team evaluating the chart, the chart provides a visual representation of overall desirability of different options. For example, based on the factors listed in the chart, the customer would likely be more likely to choose a monster truck than a drag racer.

INTERRELATIONSHIP MATRIX

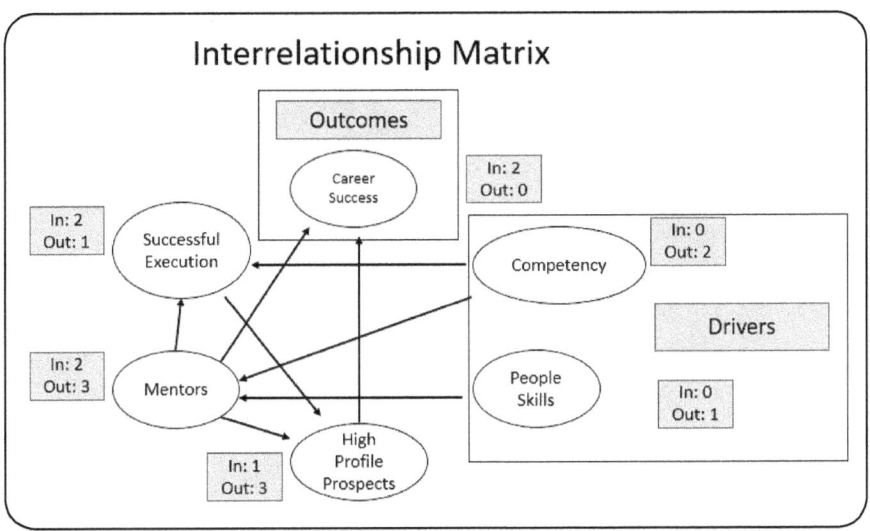

Interrelationship matrix is a way to evaluate cause and effect relationships between a group of issues, processes, or items. Through use of this matrix, issues can be evaluated in order to determine the significance of each issue as well as the causal effect each issue can have on other areas of a process or other items.

The use of both "in" and "out" arrows in the matrix helps determine levels of significance, particularly by evaluating which factors or issues have the highest number of "in" arrows, or the most factors impacting it. This helps evaluate complex problems and helps determine desired outcomes. This is a popular tool used to evaluate particularly complex problems and develop proper solutions. To create the diagram, the first step is to identify the problem and associated issues, connect issues that are interrelated or impact each other, and look at these issues to identify issues with the highest impact. The factors with the most "out" arrows typically can be identified as drivers while those with the most "in" arrows can be identified as the outcomes. This guides decision making and planning by allowing teams to know which problems or issues to target first.

ADEM STRATEGY MANAGEMENT CYCLICAL MODEL

The ADEM Strategy Management Cyclical Model (ADEM model) was developed by Dr. Mario Wallace in 2019. The ADEM model is a strategy management framework for busy leaders across industries to communicate a clear path of application from the beginning to the end of the strategy management process. The ADEM model is a high-level strategy management process that helps simplify the elements of the Balanced Scorecard (BSC) and any other strategy management tool. The model was designed to help busy leaders across industries work on detailed elements of a plan while remaining focused on the end goal. The acronym stands for the four identified phases of strategy management: Analyze, Develop, Execute, and Manage. Each phase has actionable elements that are unique to the phase and interdependent to the elements across the model.

The analysis phase consists of analyzing external market data and internal data, avoiding biases in the data, and choosing the most competitive strategic direction for the organization. The development phase consists of translating market and operational data into a concrete and actionable plan. The execution phase consists of effectively implementing a strategy into the culture of the organization through strategic alignment of its internal resources and cascading objectives to business units. The manage phase consists of aligning the reporting of the plan across an organization, conducting scheduled strategic meetings to discuss the strategic performance, and testing the hypothesis of the plan and pressure testing the plan.

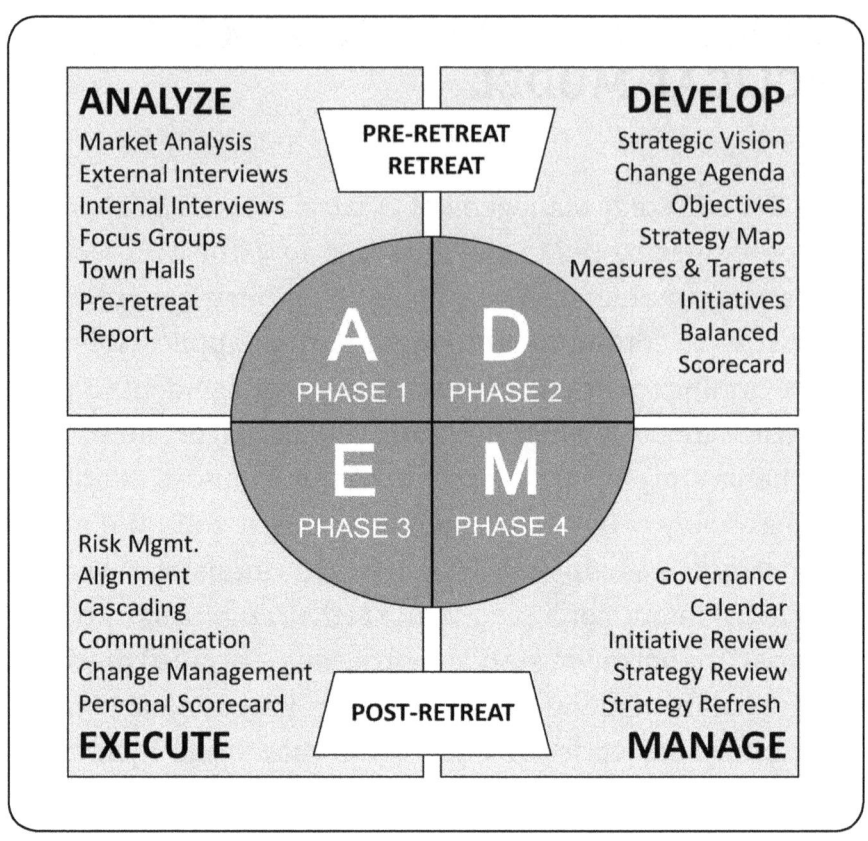

The ADEM model represents a linear progression across multiple phases and dependent elements. The elements of the ADEM model are equally important as the phases in the model. The elements consist of 20 dependent and interdependent steps and management tools that must be considered in the strategy management process. The tools are a combination of existing frameworks such as the PEST Analysis, Porter's Five Forces, Kaplan-Norton's strategy map, PROSCI's ADKAR, etcetera.

TIME HORIZONS CONE

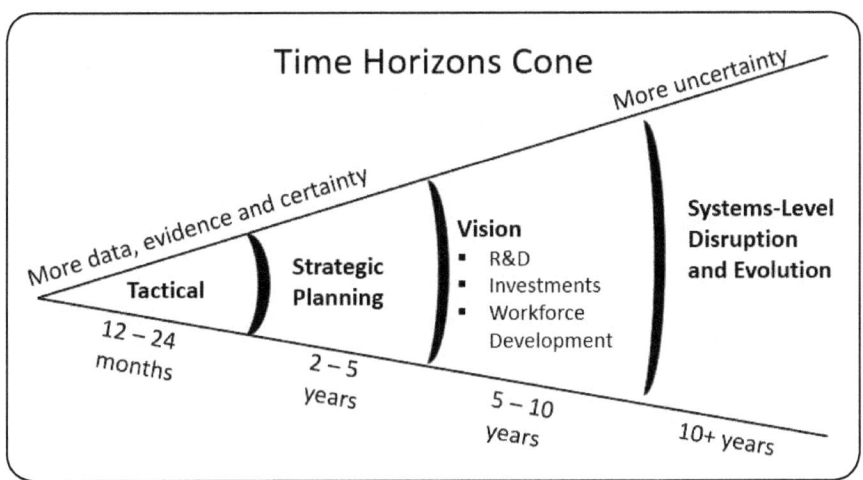

Time Horizons Cone (THC) is a framework that is designed to help leaders across industries focus on managing tactical inputs and outputs, collecting data, identifying emerging trends, developing strategies, and calculating the probabilities of various scenarios occurring in the future. The TCH offers a dual approach to strategic decision making. Leaders must simultaneously think about short- and long-term strategies when using the framework to create and manage a strategic plan. Unlike other strategic planning frameworks, the THC framework is an ongoing process of building out tactical and strategic planning action activities, and consistently collecting and analyzing fringe data and evidence that shapes the future of a firm. The THC framework helps leaders to continue moving a strategy forward, while resetting it multiple times throughout the duration of the strategy.

Amy Webb, the Chief Executive Officer of the Future Today Institute, uses the THC to educate and develop data-driven strategic planning models that focus on one to two-year action activities and plausible scenarios at the fringe of society. THC consists of four distinct categories: tactical, strategic planning, vision, and system-level disruption and evolution. The tactical category focuses on operational resources and factors that can immediately create value for a firm and its customers. In this category, there is an abundance of data to use in making tactical decisions to mobilize a firm to compete for accessible resources. Timelines, programs, and projects are relevant in this category. This is the most certain category of them all. The strategic planning category focuses on resources that shape the near future of a firm. In this category, data and evidence are based on trends that are less certain than the trends in the tactical category. The time range of the strategic planning category is between 2- to 5-years. Timelines, objectives, measures, and targets are relevant in this category. The vision category teeters on much more uncertainty and unknowns. The vision category is based on research and potential investments over a 5- to 10-year strategic horizon. Broad goals are formulated in this category that shape the near future. The system-level disruption and evolution category focus on an unknown future based on probabilities. The data and evidence in this category are based on disparate points that are somewhat random but are extremely crucial to the sustainability of a firm. This category describes the direction that a firm needs to evolve.

REVIEW QUESTIONS

1. Who is/are the author(s) of the framework?

2. What are the elements of the framework?

3. Describe the framework.

4. What is the purpose of the framework?

Strategic Frameworks

5. What are the contemporaries of the framework?

6. How to apply the framework? Please explain.

7. Example of the framework in society.

8. Is the framework still relevant today?

9. Does the framework better relate to factors of the information age or industrial age? Please explain.

10. Compare and contrast the framework to a contemporary.

11. Please apply the framework to a business solution.

ABOUT THE AUTHOR

Dr. Mario D. Wallace, President of All Things Strategic, has more than 20 years of small business consulting experience and 11 years of healthcare consulting experience. He has considerable expertise in the areas of process improvement, change management, leadership development, medical education, program instructional development, and strategic management. Dr. Wallace published the article "Four Cognitive Skills of Business Strategists" that sparked the idea for his creation of the ADEM Strategy Management Cyclical Model. The model is the first strategy management tool that simplifies the elements of the Balanced Scorecard (BSC) and any other strategy management process. He has also created the ADEM Strategic Planning Readiness Assessment, the ADEM Active-learning Instruction Model, and the OPDC Strategic Thinking Competency Assessment.

Dr. Wallace continues to serve as a strategic advisor for leaders of community hospitals, healthcare systems, academic medical centers, and small businesses. In particular, he served as a strategic advisor for leaders at the University of Arkansas for Medical Sciences (UAMS), Community Health Centers of Arkansas, the VA Hospital in Memphis, Tennessee, and multiple small businesses across the south.

Prior to starting All Things Strategic, he was the Director of the Office of Strategy Management at UAMS—the only academic medical hospital in Arkansas. He led executives at UAMS in the development of the Vision 2029 plan using the ADEM Strategy Management Cyclical Model. His strategic and operational expertise was used at UAMS to develop, cascade, and manage strategies across multiple colleges and support units. He has also developed strategic plans for Community Health Centers of Arkansas, the VA Hospital in Memphis, Tennessee, Arkansas Center for Health Improvements (ACHI), University of Arkansas at Little Rock, and multiple small businesses.

Dr. Wallace earned his bachelor's degrees in International Language and Rhetoric and Writing and his master's degree in education from the University of Arkansas at Little Rock. He earned his doctoral degree from Walden University in Business Administration Leadership. He has certifications in the Balanced Scorecard from Palladium Group, Lean Six Sigma Black Belt from Villanova University, Change Management from PROSCI, Emotional Intelligence from the Hay Group, Communication from Everything DiSC Workplace, and Facilitation from Development Demission International (DDI). Dr. Wallace is a member of the American College of Healthcare Executives (ACHE).

OUR CONSULTING SERVICES

Strategic Planning

Strategic planning is the process of analyzing market data and internal factors and making decisions to chart a path to expand markets, compete within markets, disrupt markets, and/or create a networking market. It is also about choosing a unique and valuable position rooted in systems of activities that are difficult to match. We help business owners, C-level executives, and board members define their strategy, or direction, and make decisions on allocating resources to pursue their strategy. We facilitate strategic planning retreats that include leaders and their implementation teams.

Our goal is to help clients develop plans to achieve accelerated growth of business in an era of new technological advances and hyper-competition. We also assist leaders in executing and managing their strategy.

Advising

Our advising services help professionals and organizations effectively navigate business risks and opportunities—including strategic and operational (e.g. change management, project management, and process improvement) risks—to gain and sustain competitive advantage. We apply our experience in ongoing business strategies and operations to help clients become stronger and more resilient and to make competitors irrelevant.

Assessments

Our consultants administer a wide array of assessments that will aid in personal and team development, and a systematic process for evaluating process inefficiencies and potential strategic or operational risks.

All consultants are certified in Lean Six Sigma, Wiley's Workplace DiSC, Hay Group's Emotional and Social Competency Inventory, Wallace's OPDC Strategic Thinking Assessment, and Wallace's ADEM Strategy Management Assessment.

Workshops

Our interactive workshops are facilitated by certified experts in their field and subject who collaboratively design their material to help professionals and organizations create a culture of employee engagement and strong leadership. We help professionals outperform their peers and likely beat their competition in attracting top talent.

Our interactive workshops are customizable to include activities that are applicable to all professional work environments.

Strategic Thinking

Strategic thinking is a rational decision-making process that focuses on sensing, analyzing, and reconfiguring ideas, concepts, and strategies to create new ways of doing business that differentiates a firm from its competitor. In this workshop, the facilitator discusses ways to improve one's strategic thinking skills and teaches practical strategic thinking methods to maximize business decisions. Participants complete an OPDC (operation, planning, discovery, and creation) strategic thinking assessment to learn their own strategic thinking capabilities and to create an action plan to strengthen their strategic thinking skills.

Becoming a Strategically Aligned Business

The facilitator uses concepts from Kaplan-Norton's Balanced Scorecard framework to educate participants on the elements of a strategy-focused firm. Participants gain knowledge and practical application of aligning a firm's internal resources, translating strategy across a firm, and creating personal scorecards for their employees. Participants will also learn the role that culture plays in creating a strategy-focused organization.

Generational Differences

The facilitator lays out the differences amongst generations using historical elements that support each generation's beliefs, politics, or values. The facilitator also teaches strategies to leverage positive interactions between generations.

Positive Interpersonal Communication

The facilitator lays out the 7 elements of positive communication using the Dr. Julien Mirivel's Model of Positive Communication. Participants learn how to engage customers, co-workers, partners, and business partners in a positive interaction. Participants complete the DiSC Communication Style Assessment and learn their preferred communication style and how to determine the communication styles of others. Participants learn communication strategies to create a positive working environment.

Emotional Intelligence

The facilitator lays out the four elements of Emotional Intelligence (EI)- self-awareness, self-management, organizational awareness, and relationship management- in an interactive, team-based learning setting. The facilitator teaches strategies for enhancing participant's knowledge and application of EI elements to evaluate personal strengths as well as opportunities for development.

Change Management

The facilitator explains the principles of Change Management using relevant industry-specific case studies. The facilitator teaches core elements that affect organizational change and individual change. Participants learn the five barriers of change and how to leverage them to mitigate resistance. Participants learn how to develop a sponsor roadmap, a communication plan, and a corrective action plan. Participants learn strategies to mitigate employee resistance.

Team Building

The facilitator lays out the elements for fostering a sociable and collaborative workplace to increase productivity. The participants learn strategies to enhance their interpersonal relationships with co-workers to create team spirit, fun, and motivation. The participants also learn strategies to engage the workforce to stimulate innovation, creation, and friendly competition.

Patient Error Prevention

To succeed in healthcare, it is imperative that your institution adopts a culture of safety. This workshop is facilitated by a certified HPI (health process improvement) professional. The facilitator teaches the importance of safety as a top priority. We first analyze current error rates through review of patient complaints, surveys, and sentinel events. Once we have a baseline of safety in your institution, we start the conversation of how to improve this level of safety. We collaborate with administrative and physician leadership, while also including front line staff.

OUR PRODUCTS

Books

Strategy Is Spelled ADEM—Strategy Is Spelled ADEM is the Holy Grail of strategy management. The ADEM Strategy Management Cyclical Model is a high-level strategy management process that helps simplify the elements of the strategy management process. The model was designed to help busy leaders across industries work on detailed elements of a strategic plan while remaining focused on the end goal. The ADEM acronym stands for the four identified phase of strategy management: Analyze, Develop, Execute, and Manage. Strategy Is Spelled ADEM is available on Amazon.

The Unstoppable Leader—The Unstoppable Leader is a practical guide and toolkit for leaders who desire to be dynamic and competitive in their approach to business solutions. The book introduces leaders to strategic frameworks and operational tools to help them determine the best competitive approach for their business. Leaders also learn the history, purpose, and application of some of these frameworks and tools, used by top business strategists and process improvement practitioners. The Unstoppable Leader is available on Amazon.

Self-Study Courses

Strategy for Teaching Hospitals—Strategy Made Simple for Teaching Hospitals is a self-study course that focuses on strategy development and managing a strategic plan in an academic medical center. This course uses a case study from a teaching hospital to break down the phases and elements of strategy management and to educate leaders in teaching hospitals on the do's and don'ts of strategic planning. The course also introduces readers to a new approach to the PEST analysis. This course includes a quiz and self-graded questions designed to enhance reader's knowledge and understanding of strategy management. Strategy Made Simple for Teaching Hospitals is available at https://allthingsstrategic.biz/contact/.

Strategy for Busy Executives -Strategy for Busy Executives is a self-study course that focuses on the application of the strategy management process using the phases of the ADEM Strategy Management Cyclical Model. This course includes a reading that explains the practical approach to the ADEM Readiness Assessment along with the assessment itself. It also includes a step-by-step scope of work guide to walk you through the strategic planning process. This course includes a quiz and self-graded questions designed to enhance reader's knowledge and understanding of strategy management. Strategy Made Simple for Teaching Hospitals is available at https://allthingsstrategic.biz/contact/.

Games

STRATE-O—STRATE-O is a 2-in-one board and card game set that is designed to challenge and enhance a leader's knowledge and application of strategy management frameworks and operational tools. The game set includes a board game and a card game. Both games target a leader's analytical, critical, and strategic thinking. The goal of STRATEG-O is to help develop a leader's cognition for complex, strategic business solutions. Inquire about the STRATE-O leadership board game at https://allthingsstrategic.biz/contact/.

FreezeMe—FreezeMe is a competitive team building sport for leaders across all industries. The sport is well-structured and organized and it is like football in that two teams compete against each other on a court that is measured in yards. The sport includes positions such as coaches, players, and referees. FreezeMe offers an interactive team building experience like no other.

FreezeMe can be played as a single team building sport or it can be combined with the Everything DiSC Workplace.® FreezeMe is best leveraged as a team building activity when it is combined with the Everything DiSC Workplace.® Everything DiSC Workplace ® is a personalized learning experience that can benefit every person in the organization—regardless of title or position, department or function—by building more productive and effective relationships at work. We combine the Everything DiSC Workplace® in a classroom setting along with FreezeMe to give you a fun team building experience. Inquire about the FreezeMe team building sport for leaders at https://allthingsstrategic.biz/contact/.

Assessments

ADEM Readiness Assessment—The ADEM Readiness Assessment is a self-assessment instrument that assesses competencies associated with 16 key elements of the ADEM Strategy Management Cyclical Model. The ADEM Strategy Management Cyclical Model organizes the strategy management process into four easy-to-follow phases: 1) Analyze, 2) Develop, 3) Execute, and 4) Manage. Each phase has actionable elements that are dependent on the phase and interdependent to the other elements across the model. Inquire about the ADEM Readiness Assessment at https://allthingsstrategic.biz/contact/.

OPDC Strategic Thinking Assessment—The OPDC (e.g. Operations, Planning, Discovery, and Creation) Strategic Thinking Assessment is an instrument that is used to assess the strategic thinking competencies of leaders. Strategic thinking is a rational decision-making process that focuses on gathering the right data, avoiding biases, and doing activities that differentiate firms from its competitors. Leaders are expected to manage the day-to-day operations, plan for tomorrow, innovate products and services, and create strategies to sustain a competitive advantage to advance their business priorities. As a result, leaders MUST enhance their strategic thinking competencies to remain viable in today's hyper competitive markets. Inquire about the OPDC Strategic Thinking Assessment at https://allthingsstrategic.biz/contact/.

www.ingramcontent.com/pod-product-compliance
Lightning Source LLC
Chambersburg PA
CBHW070124100426
42744CB00010B/1917